NATIONAL MONUMENT ESTABLISHED

Aztec Ruins National Monument established in 1923 and is 318 acres.

Bandelier National Monument established in 1916 and is 32737 acres.

Capulin Volcano National Monument established in 1916 and is 793 acres.

El Malpais National Monument established in 1987 and is 114277 acres.

El Morro National Monument established in 1906 and is 1278 acres.

Fort Union National Monument established in 1954 and is 721 acres.

Gila Cliff Dwellings National Monument established in 1907 and is 533 acres.

Petroglyph National Monument established in 1990 and is 7100 acres.

Salinas Pueblo Missions National Monument established in 1909 and is 1071 acres.

Tent Rocks National Monument established in 2001 and is 4114 acres.

White Sands National Monument established in 1933 and is 143733 acres.

SANDIA MOUNTAINS

© William Stone

© Kevin Sheilds

Sandia Peak Tramway

© Laurence Parent

© William Stone

ALBUQUERQUE

Albuquerque

Rio Grande River in Coronado State Park

© Jonathan Meyers

Old Town Plaza with luminarias

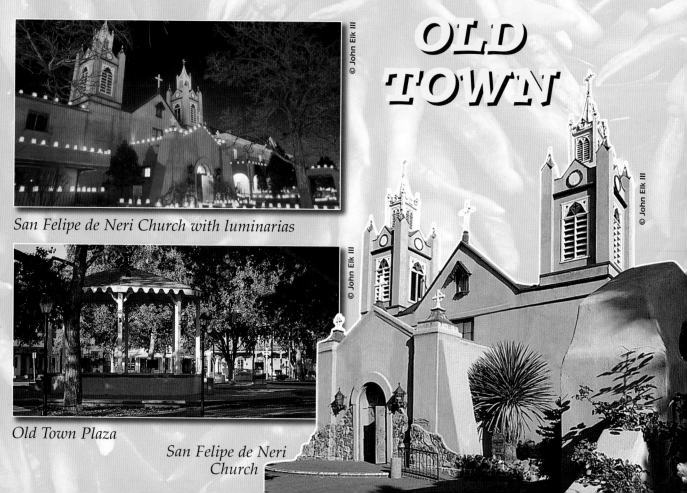

© John Elk III

San Felipe de Neri Church with luminarias

Old Town Plaza

© John Elk III

© John Elk III

San Felipe de Neri
Church

OLD TOWN

The Albuquerque Balloon Fiesta® is a beautiful event that attracts hundreds of thousands of spectators every October. The Albuquerque Balloon Fiesta® has hundreds of the most beautifully colored and shaped balloons that one will ever see. The Sandia Mountains and the Rio Grande nearby offer a spectacular backdrop to this event.

Albuquerque Balloon Fiesta®

Hot Air Balloons
at Angel Fire

© Deb Friedrichs

© K.L Thompson

© K.D. Dittlinger

*Albuquerque Balloon
Fiesta*®

© R.E. Lindsey

© Gary Rassmussen

*Hot Air Balloon
near Farmington*

*Hot Air Ballooning in
White Sands National Monument*

7

SANTA FE

Town Plaza

Governors Palace

© Bruce Elliot

St. Francis Mission

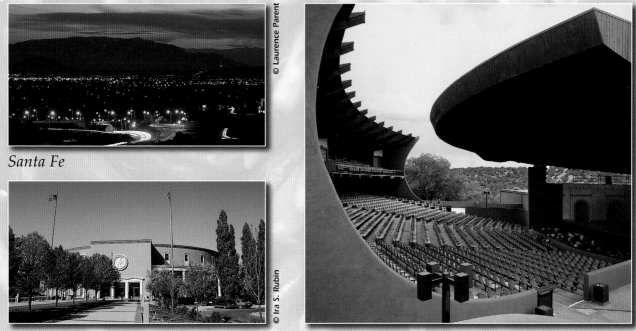

© Laurence Parent

Santa Fe

© Ira S. Rubin

State Capital

Santa Fe Opera

© Laurence Parent

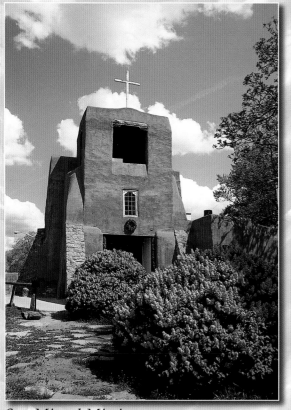

Authentic Santa Fe architecture

San Miguel Mission

Camel Rock

Loretto Chapel

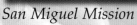

The spiral staircase inside Loretto Chapel

Chama River

© Tom Till

Upper Falls in Frijoles Canyon. Bandelier National Monument

*Soda Dam in the
Jemez Mountains*

*Kasha Katuwa Tent Rocks
National Monument*

Asters and Chamisa near Abiquiu

Wheeler Peak in Sangre de Cristo Mountains

Eagle Nest Lake

© William Stone

Capulin Volcano National Monument

Fishing on the Cimarron River

Rafting the Rio Grande

© Dick Dietrich

© Deb Friedrichs

Fort Union National Monument

© Gary Rassmussen

Rio Grand Gorge near Taos

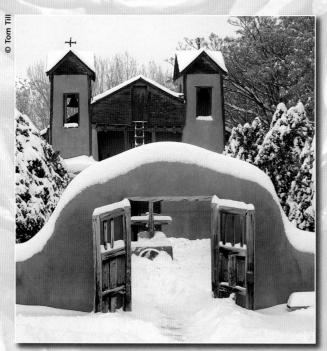

Sanctuario de Chimayo

Inside of El Sanctuario de Chimayo

Taos Pueblo

San Francisco de Asis Church in Ranchos de Taos

Taos Pueblo

The "old church" steeple at Taos Pueblo

© K.L. Thompson

Puye Cliff dwellings

© Gary Rassmussen

St. Augustine Church at Isleta Pueblo

San Ildefonso Pueblo

© Grace Davies

Bandelier National Monument

Chaco Canyon National Historic Park

Aztec National Monument

Pecos National Historic Park

Gila Cliff Dwellings National Monument

Salinas Pueblo Missions National Monument

© Tom Till

© Bob Young

Laguna Pueblo

Gallup

*Continental
Divide*

CONTINENTAL DIVIDE
INDIAN JEWELRY
Gift Shop
ARTS

ROUTE **66**

Grants

Laguna

ALBUQUERQ

*La Ventana Arch
in El Malpais National Monument*

Acoma Pueblo

© Bob & Suzanne Clemenz

© Tom Till

© Deb Friedrichs

© Dick Dietrich

ta Fe

Tucumcari

Santa Rosa

Petroglyph National Monument

© Laurence Parent

© Tom Till

© Dick Dietrich

© Gary Rassmussen

Valley of Fires

© Kevin Sheilds

Large Array Antennae

*Bosque del Apache
National Wildlife
Refuge, near Socorro*

TRINITY SITE
WHERE
THE WORLD'S FIRST
NUCLEAR DEVICE
WAS EXPLODED ON
JULY 16, 1945

ERECTED 1965
WHITE SANDS MISSILE RANGE
J. FREDERICK THORLIN
MAJOR GENERAL U.S. ARMY
COMMANDING

*Trinity Site, location of the
worlds first Nuclear Bomb*

© Laurence Parent

© Laurence Parent

Three Rivers Petroglyph site with Sierra Blanca Peak

© Bruce Finchum

Elephant Butte Lake

© Laurence Parent

Cloudcroft

© Bill Baker

International Space Hall of Fame in Alamogordo

© D.B. Friedrichs

© J.C. Leacock

*Yucca in White Sands
National Monument*

© Cynthia Spence

*Carlsbad Caverns
National Park,
a World Heritage Site*

© Deb Friedrichs

*Bottomless Lake
State Park
near Roswell*

Organ
Mountains

© Kevin Sheilds

City of Rocks
State Park

© Clay Martin

Las Cruces

© Kevin Sheilds

© Tom Till

© J.C. Leacock

*Sawtooth Range
in Cibola National Forest*

El Morro National Monument

© Willard Clay

Zuni Mountains

© Gary Rassmussen

*Cumbres & Toltec
Scenic Railway*

© Tom Till

Red Rock State Park

© Clay Martin

Bisti Wilderness

31

Roadrunner

Gila Monster

New Mexico Wildlife

Desert Coyote

Jack Rabbit

Hummingbird